THE STC

SuAndi

THE STORY OF M

OBERON BOOKS
LONDON

WWW.OBERONBOOKS.COM

The Story of M was first published in 2002 by artBlacklive, Black Arts Alliance, Manchester, UK.

It was published in *The Routledge Drama Anthology and Source book: From Modernism to Contemporary Performance,* 2010.

This single edition published in 2017 by Oberon Books Ltd
521 Caledonian Road, London N7 9RH
Tel: +44 (0) 20 7607 3637 / Fax: +44 (0) 20 7607 3629
e-mail: info@oberonbooks.com
www.oberonbooks.com

A catalogue record for this book is available from the British Library.

PB ISBN: 9781786821157
E ISBN: 9781786821164

Cover artwork *The Reader* is generously donated and copyright held by Faith Bebbington / www.faithbebbington.co.uk

Printed and bound by 4edge Limited, Essex, UK.
eBook conversion by Lapiz Digital Services, India.

Visit www.oberonbooks.com to read more about all our books and to buy them. You will also find features, author interviews and news of any author events, and you can sign up for e-newsletters so that you're always first to hear about our new releases.

Contents

SuAndi

This publication owes thanks to people who have supported my work over the good and hard times that all writers face:

Dr Deirdre Osborne, whose determination has driven this publication.

Dr Corinne Fowler

Emeritus Professor Mick Wallis

Professors Geraldine Harris & Elaine Aston

George Spender of Oberon Books

Professor Graham Mort most especially for his patience in guiding the final poetry edits and I also want to acknowledge Dr Muli Amaye and Peter Kalu.

Dedicated to my friends & sistahs
Director Emeritus Dr Barbara Nicholson
Dr Chamion Caballero
Carla Henry
And especially
Kirk (Brosun) Washington Jnr. 1974-2016

In memory of my late family
Mum, Dad, and Malcolm

I wrote M following a mediocre production that closed with homage to white women who had endured racism following their interracial marriages. Lois Keidan felt it was the strongest section and encouraged me to write more, as fact is always more interesting. Forty minutes into my return journey to Manchester I'd done as advised with tears running down my face. It took very little more writing to complete.

M has been seen by audiences across the UK and in Ireland, Germany, San Francisco, Atlanta, Cleveland and Columbus Ohio

Acknowledgments

Commissioners: Keidan/Ugwu (ICA)

Additional visuals: Ronald Fraser-Munroe
and © Bert Hardy Picture Post

M's nurse: Carla Henry

Previous cast; Tracy Vidal, Hanna Adu-Boateng, Crystal James (Canada), and Christiana Fonthes (Goldsmiths, University of London, 19 January 2017).

Directing advice original production: Bush Hartsorn

Technical advice: Steve Bryan

The Story of M has been performed all over the world including the following venues.

- artBlacklive-Celeb' Manchester Festival
- Battersea Arts Centre London
- Black Theatre Festival, Atlanta
- Black Theatre Festival, West Yorkshire Playhouse
- Bluecoat Arts Centre Liverpool
- Cheltenham Literature Festival
- City Of Drama Manchester
- Creative Workshop Projects – Cleveland USA
- Dartington Arts College
- Ferris Hill and St Giles – Cleveland USA; Indianapolis, USA
- Focus on Women Arts Festival – British Columbia
- Green Room – Manchester
- Greenwich Black Arts Festival London
- Horsham Arts Centre, Horsham
- ICA London
- Kumba Bristol
- Lancaster University
- Loughborough University
- Martin Luther King Jr Complex – Ohio USA
- Manchester City of Drama
- Mix Mexico
- Nottingham Playhouse
- NOW Festival Nottingham
- Peterborough Arts Centre
- Republic of Ireland 7-day tour African Cultural Project
- San Francisco International Arts Festival
- Simba Project Greenwich London
- The Castle Wellingborough
- The Citadel St Helens
- Yaa Asantewaa London

I began my professional writing life in 1985 as a staff member at Cultureword working alongside Lemn Sissay who was my first mentor and at the same time I joined Manchester's first Black women's poetry collective Blackscribe, together we were the front runners in performance poetry.

I never imagined that I could really make a career simply out of writing and in truth I haven't. My work through collaboration with the dynamic artists of National Black Arts Alliance has taken me along exciting and varied creative journeys including writing the *Mary Seacole* libretto. I have also enjoyed prominence as a keynote speaker and panelist in the UK and across Europe, Brazil, British Columbia, Singapore, South and West Africa and North America.

I have been "gonged", receiving the OBE (Officer of the Order of the British Empire 1999), I have been an Honorary Creative Writer Fellow at Leicester University since 2014 and in 2015 I received a Doctor of Letters, Honorary Degree from Lancaster University

Never has one owed so much to so many
(It's a writer's prerogative to play with words!)

I have had so many people men, women of all hues, and heritages who have held my hand I could fill this book with their names. I hope that in turn I have been a mentor to others.

"I closed my eyes during your performance and could see clearly the images created by your words.
I could never do what you do, get up and perform like that, I wouldn't have the courage."
Edward Bond, Playwright

"a stunning performance... SuAndi's script was rich, inventive with generous humour...her performance was flawless! Truly an autobiographical gem for theatre for the 21st Century!!"
Rhodessa Jones, Artistic Director, San Francisco International Arts Festival

SuAndi speaks with authoritative eloquence in a show that looks at biographical matters most people are often too afraid to examine. Her style is refined.
Carl Palmer, *Manchester Evening News*

Mothertext: Restoring the Mixed Matrilineal Routes to *Heritage*

By Deirdre Osborne
(Goldsmiths, University of London)

Contexts

SuAndi's monodrama[1], *The Story of M* earns its place in the tradition of women writers and performers who have moved cultural narratives and social perspectives in new and radical directions.[2] Through traversing the performative[3] modes of poetic theatre and theatricalised poetics, SuAndi's creative work highlights the porous relationship between forms of textual enunciation – on and off the page – as read to oneself, as recited, as spoken-word event, or as staged drama. Her transformative uses of genre offer a distinctive artistic voice to the wealth of experiences not characteristically at the centre of British cultural representations, such as mixed-race or black women, lone mothers, orphaned children, elderly people, those with disability, low paid workers, and a range of survivors of exploitation, discrimination, and abuse.[4] In many respects, this might suggest a grim litany, but SuAndi creates irascible and charismatic personae to convey the multiple aspects to these individuals' psychosocial portraits, to wrest them from generalisation or stereotype.[5]

The Story of M was commissioned in 1994 by the visionary Live Arts programmers Lois Keidan and Catherine Ugwu, for the Institute of Contemporary Arts at a time when British-born writers of African descent were beginning to assert their artistic presence in mainstream culture, while maintaining strong grassroots connections. Although influenced by the migratory sensibility of post-war generations (and their linguistic and performance innovations that forever changed Anglophone poetics), the indigene perspectives in this late-twentieth-century creative work were tailored towards representing the particular experiences of growing up Black[6] in Britain – for which there was no representational aesthetic tradition.[7] The racialised and gendered politics of arts subsidy in this period defined the routes that many writers and performers took in realising their creative aims, a context in which SuAndi became an arts activist and advocate.[8] Forming a creative and critical mass to recognise black people's expressive agencies was key, for 'One of the consequences of the genesis of pernicious stereotypes equating dark skin with inferiority – Europe's most enduring act of creativity – has been that it was not counteracted by an *equivalent* body of material' representing the perspectives of people labelled in this way. (Osborne 2016:27)

The Story of M adds to this restorative continuum. Furthermore, as a monodrama it presents the audience with only one option, a solo performer, by which to 'receive' the text in its performance, or as narrated on the page – this figure is both agent and authority. W.B. Worthen suggests that, 'Poetic drama imagines a recalibration of the *agency* of writing in the process of theatre.' (2010:43) SuAndi as writer and performer of her mother's life inhabits the theatrical agency and dramatic agency simultaneously, (in acting M) to make M's narrative, 'stageworthy, capable of being used to create meaningful action in the *scene* of the theatre.' (Worthen 2010: 56) Notably, SuAndi does not simply challenge realism on verbal grounds in this poetic theatre piece. Her monodrama's performance becomes, to use Worthen's definition, 'a significant critical *act* in that larger *scene*, the changing scene of social life. The theatre's makers and audiences [as a result] learn to read, to do, and to see differently.' (2010:56)

The Story of M demands multiple levels of awareness with regards to its representational range: the historically specific prejudices dictating how mothers who crossed racial and marital lines were viewed, the trans-historic racist reflex in social attitudes they and their children experience, and as Chamion Caballero (2012) points out, that the norms of daily life were often an affirming counterpoint to institutional and socio-cultural exclusions. In *The Story of M*, SuAndi achieves her most stunning reconfiguration of the expectations that have become historically 'attached' to her maternal subject matter,[9] while implicitly subjecting to scrutiny, the meta-context of the British theatre complex (in relation to the roles of and for black and mixed-race women), and the multiple generic possibilities by which to articulate alternatives to dominant cultural models.[10]

11

For the first time, in this volume, SuAndi also offers a series of her previously unpublished 'Mother Poems'. [The companion poem to *The Story of M* is undoubtedly 'All Your Family' (p.69) – an anthem to treasuring the tenacity of single motherhood and mixed families.] Their inclusion extends the matrilineal sweep of *The Story of M*, of its sole speaker M (and all she symbolises) to collect heart-rending, timeless, moments in womanhood where the mother is the poetic compass by which all bearings are set within each poem, bar one.[11] These are not merely nostalgic or sentimentalising works, but engender a simultaneous 'mother's – daughter's' perspective, rescuing this relationship from between the lines of literature and its institutional silencing – where as Adrienne Rich identifies – it has been 'minimized and trivialized in the annals of patriarchy' (1977:226), to craft a maternal aesthetics, a Mothertext. Mothertext I propose, to apply Abigail L. Palko's definition of a maternal imaginary, 'deconstructs socially imposed maternal norms' (2016:2) and recognises the centrality of the mother-daughter relationship to women's lives. The Mothertext is one that moves from mother to daughter standpoint effortlessly, where there are no boundaries in perception: from a daughter's reflections upon her mother; (or, as SuAndi imaginatively *re*constructs hers) to a mother's on her daughter; and beyond this, in an application to daughters of other mothers and mothers of other daughters. In the poems, 'Everlasting' (p.70) and 'Nandos' (p.63) she represents what Rich describes as the bequest of the mother-daughter relationship, 'a kind of strength which can only be one woman's gift to another, the bloodstream of our inheritance'. (1977:246)

SuAndi's performance of *The Story of M* – where the mother M is 'acted' by the daughter who 'acts' as her mother – illustrates Kristin M. Langellier's observation that 'personal narrative performance *constitutes* identities and experience, producing and reproducing that to which it refers.' (1999:128) The matrilineal bodily identifications in both the monodrama and the Mother Poems provide a sound riposte to Lacan's mirror stage. Rich's concept, 'matrophobia', the fear of becoming one's mother, is encapsulated and problematised by the performative arc of *The Story of M* through to its ultimate coup-de-théâtre, which both acknowledges and separates mother and daughter, acted self from actual self. As Rich writes, 'Our personalities seem dangerously to blur and overlap with our mothers'; and, in a desperate attempt to know where mother ends and daughter begins, we perform radical surgery.' (1977:236) Enhanced throughout by projected visual material, in its staging, what has been a seemingly 'assimilated' dramatic text (through costume, props, set, acting, speaking, supernumerary actor, lighting) is denaturalized, and actual life is restored – as declared by SuAndi who addresses the audience as herself in the final spoken text. As she points out in an interview, 'I lose myself in this performance [...] I did it in Manchester once – and I watched the video and thought "heavens, I look dreadful, I look so tired." When I changed from being my mother to being SuAndi, I looked fine.' (Fuchs 2006:211)

The poem 'The Twin' (p.65) similarly explores this identification as the speaker leads the reader through an account of cleaving to and splitting from the mother's body (its polysemy of both parting and joining) as a journey to self-acceptance. The poem opens 'in media res' where the reader must follow a perplexing route to the final stanza.

> My mother had one
> just the same
> Not identical
> naturally
> thankfully

SuAndi's paratactical writing technique features here – as it does in *The Story of M* – to convey a sense of anecdotal reminiscence which is conveyed by an archness of tone and self parody. The poem's persona's rejection of sharing her mother's physicality is played out in disdain, endurance, sacrifice, and denial – in contrast to her mother's indulgent jouissance. Ultimately she finds herself in her mother, through an inescapable bodily truth that is fecund and female.

> And in spite – yes! –
> in spite of all my efforts
> the bulge that rests arrogantly
> beneath my breasts
> is twinned in shape and form
> to the stomach-bulge belly
> of my mother's.

The acerbic wit with which she delivers her subjects' human frailties and vulnerabilities, setbacks and triumphs, does not shy away from the consequences of life's harsh aspects. While her poetic and dramatic speakers may face emotional capsizing – crucially – they do not capitulate to the adversities. In 'Hands' (p.62) and 'Lady Making' (p.64) SuAndi employs a central controlled image of the mother's hands as particular testimony to a mother's toil to survive and make a future for her daughter. Their resilience and survival is projected as continuing beyond the borders of her poems, even as exhaustion or utter grief is voiced. In both poems, the maternal speaker's hands are poetic conceits to articulate bleak experiences of a lack of valuing of maternal labour by society, but acutely observed by her beneficiary, her daughter. The scope of reference is simultaneously intimate and universally applicable, implying the unspoken means of witnessing and transmitting history between women. No matter how isolated or alone the poetic voice appears to be, there is no doubting that the context in which the speaker is positioned is one girded by a conscious sense of heritage that is both local and personal, yet concurrently a part of collective history. SuAndi employs this 'subjective' approach throughout her poetry and with *The Story of M* illustrates Theodor Adorno's point about the aesthetics of subjectivity – 'What is subjectively expressed does not need to resemble the expressing subject. In many instances what is expressed will be precisely what the expressing subject is not'. (1997:276)

Mixed Messages

In addition to creating a compelling crosstalk between drama, performance, and spoken-word poetry, SuAndi places interracial and mixed experiences at the heart of the reclamation of hidden 'herstories'.[12] However, while distinctive commentaries on her work offer incisive and provoking analyses[13], there exist lacunae within the range of interpretations that confirms the need to develop a conceptual and critical lexicon, in order to meet the epistemological challenges to representation, that mixedness and dramatic-poetics produce.

As witness to multiple productions of *The Story of M*, Elaine Aston offers invaluable performance analyses of its significance to feminist theatre practice, identifying how the transformative moment, (the slide of M) is premised upon commonly held, racially stereotyping assumptions:

It is not until the last slide is shown, and the audience sees a photograph of Margaret for the first time, that it is clear that Margaret was white. At this point, SuAndi steps out of character [...] For the spectator, especially the white spectator, what is demonstrated through the Gestus of the slide is an assumption that the victim of racial abuse must be black, not white. (2003:144)

Aston returns to this aspect in a later essay where she rethinks the maternal through performing the loss of the mother.

audiences tend to be visibly stunned by the white mother [...], shocked out of the way in which they have presumed to already know Margaret as a black mother. I have seen *M* on different occasions and have got to know SuAndi in a way that has enabled me to get 'close' to this story – but even knowing as I do, I still feel the effects of Margaret's whiteness. (2007:135)

Aston's examples of audiences' reactions to performances of *The Story of M* (ethnic or class compositions are not indicated) illustrate how this monodrama can make an audience refuse the terms of allegiance to prior assumptions (prejudices, labels, stereotypes). Robert Crawshaw's deft semantic and thematic analysis also writes of the audience member as, 'Like the wedding guest in Coleridge's *Ancient Mariner*, we are positioned as outsiders, the members of the general public who make value-judgements about others and who are now being challenged' (2009:10). In these accounts of audience perceptions (Aston and Crawshaw both imply white audiences), the white critic becomes once more the central focaliser while acknowledging their outsider status in a narrative tradition where, as Aston has observed, 'it is exceptional for a black woman to speak a white woman's experience.' (2007:135) As Gad Kaynor argues the success of the communication between a solo performer and their audience 'depends, more than in any other performance, on these spectators' ability to enact the implied spectator, namely, to internalize his/her reality convention and react accordingly' (2000:54). Both critics unwittingly reproduce the customary critical reticence to foreground *metis/isse* experience in cultural representation.

SuAndi's work releases M's family from those historical labels signifying censure, rejection and devaluing that operated to produce social shame. An audience is 'found out' in their responses to the slide of M at the end of the piece and (perhaps) shamed by the skin-deep 'misreading' they might have held, up to that point. In the context of this representational manoeuvre, feeling shame is not necessarily negative, but can be viewed as a reforming state of responsiveness, a rebirth of perceptions and conceptual boundaries. As Ahmed argues, 'shame requires an identification with the other who, as witness, returns the subject to itself. The view of this other is the view that I have taken on in relation to myself; I see myself *as if I were* this other.' (2014:106), to which Aston offers unwitting testimony when she discloses, 'I still feel the effects of Margaret's whiteness.' This perceptual mobilising can be linked to Howard Barker's manifesto in *Arguments For A Theatre*, where he states that the audience (which holds true for the reader too) 'is invited to discard its normal assumptions about the manner in which reality is reproduced… not the reiteration of common knowledge but a dislocation of perceptions' where 'the writer and the actor conspire to lure the mind into the unknown, the territory of possible changed perception.' (1993: 29, 37)

While Jayne Ifekwunigwe's six-point ethnographic framework for re-considering mixedness (in more complex and respectful ways than has been customary in phenotypic classifications), does present an integrative and interrogative model of working with testimony, it still participates in a discursive field on mixedness that is dominated by the social sciences.[14] The data collecting facticity leads to generating narratives of adversity (arising from unequal social power relations), that tend to remain the predominant means for displaying the social scientific findings – even as these can have a reforming intention. In contrast, it is frequently through the literary and dramatic disciplines, that such narratives and constraining measures are liberated by the limitless possibilities of the imagination's creative representational facility.

While mixedness as represented in literature, has generated textual and performance innovations (and in particular thematically infused young people's fiction)[15] in British culture, mixedness can also serve as an acceptable racialised concession for white-dominant, neo-liberal culture – irrespective of writers' wishes or intentions. Gabriella Beckles-Raymond records, 'the dominant media representation of the mixed-race woman suggests that there is racial harmony in Britain' whereas, 'this "masquerade" actually obscures inequalities and social injustices.' (2014:65)[16] The intersectionality of masquerade and passing, can tailor perceptions as to who gains admission to canonising circles and cultural legitimation. This remains a factor in mapping British literary value. In some critical circles, advantages can be perceived according to 'the hierarchy employed in colorism' which Angela P. Harris explains, 'is usually the same one that governs racism: light skin is prized over dark skin'. (2008:54)

Skin-deep readings have recently comprised a point of debate in the UK with the charge of 'politically black' being applied to women known for path-breaking work in developing the discourses and practices to articulate black British feminist writing.[17] Some of the neo-millennial generation identifying as Black British, now question the claim of mixed or brown women to this self-terming, a stance that recalls US categories of hypo-descent and when aligned with cultural elitism, produces uncomfortable assessments such as Irenosen Okojie's of Zadie Smith and Monica Ali: 'Both studied at Oxbridge, and both are of mixed race. What does this say to black and Asian writers: do you have to have an elite education and a white parent for the publishing industry to be interested?' (*The Guardian* 2014)

On this point, SuAndi is unequivocal in her assertion when, in closing *The Story of M*, she routs the 'tragic mulata' legacy, the mixed heritage 'confusion' myth, and the essentialism of 'Black' as comprising a totalising signifier or contingent upon dark skin tone. The text proclaims a migratory composite inheritance across borders of race and nation, to produce a cohered sense of self.

> I know exactly who I am –
> I am a Black woman
> A mixed race woman.
> [...]
> ...a Nigerian daughter
> [...]
> ...the daughter
> of a Liverpool woman of Irish descent.
> (p.55)

Behind the text

As Aston suggests, SuAndi's monodrama enables a consideration of what it is 'to be moved to think the maternal inside, rather than outside (white), histories of race, class and nation'. (2007:135) From the late-Victorian period, the anxieties concerning Empire maintenance were aligned with fortifying racial purity which became the responsibility accorded to white women, through bearing and raising Anglo-Saxon racial stock. This cast imperial motherhood as both maternity and mission. While anxieties surrounding miscegenation underpinned British colonial rule and especially the control of white women in the colonies, in the imperial heartland of the United Kingdom, genetic admixture has been a reality since the Roman occupation in ancient Britannia. The presence of black troops from the US and the British colonies during WWII left a legacy of interracial relationships and a generation of 'brown babies' who were frequently placed in adoption and fostering institutions. Although there had always been mixed children in British history, these wartime children, frequently born out of wedlock shifted the moral censure in a new direction. It cast doubt upon the propriety of married interracial couples as well as unmarried mothers.

M inherits the whole weight of this historical mother blame (working-class women were vilified as unfit and to be instructed by middle-class women, often spinsters) as a manifestation of misogyny towards the maternal.[18] The historian Laura Tabili's insightful research into documents about the interracial settlements and relationships in maritime communities of the 20s, 30s and 40s in Britain's port cities (M is Liverpudlian) concludes that in daily life, 'there is little evidence to support elite assumptions that wives of Black men were uniformly women "of a very low type," or were so defined by their neighbours'. Furthermore, 'women and interracial families were sources of order and stability, bridging and thereby blurring the racial boundaries dividing white and Black working people.' (1996:182-3) What interracial relationships did do was to threaten the ideology that sustained imperial power and its plural inequalities and hierarchies related to gender, class and race. While *The Story of M* centralises a particular post-war family make up of a white Liverpudlian Irish-heritage wife and a black Nigerian husband, it should also be remembered that black women married white Englishmen, and that interracial offspring could go onto form unions with other interracial partners or further distinct ethnic groups outside the white / black racial category. In this fluid process, racialised boundaries could shift across the generations where, 'Black and white working people could be as bound together by kinship as divided by race.' (Tabili 1996:184)[19]

Such kinship is to be found in Ngozi Onwurah's affecting auto/biographical film, *The Body Beautiful* (1990)[20] where, in one particular scene as Ifekwunigwe describes, Onwurah 'declares her allegiance to her White English mother'. She quotes Onwurah's words which, re-quoted here, share the bodily recognition processes and indebtedness that SuAndi's work also articulates.

> A child is made in its parents' image. But to a world that sees only in Black and White, I was made in the image of my father. Yet, she has moulded me, created the curves and contours of my life, coloured the innermost details of my being. She has fought for me, protected me [...] She lives inside of me and cannot be separated. I may not be reflected in her image, but my mother is mirrored in my soul. I am my mother's daughter for the rest of my life. (Onwurah 1990, qtd in Ifekwunigwe 1997:147)

Jackie Kay's homage, not just in her classic work *The Adoption Papers* (poetically representing birth and adoptive mothers and their child's voices) but in a recent tribute to her white mother, follows the same matrilineal claim.

> My magnificent mum [...] A glimpse into her past is a glimpse into my future. Her possible selves. My heart sings looking at her here [...] Now, aged 85 she calls me her second skin, her heart of hearts, her other self. If we hadn't met I would have come to find you, she says. You are as close as if I had given birth to you myself, she says.
> https://www.theguardian.com/books/2016/mar/05/writers-mothers-photographs-carol-ann-duffy

The psychic mirroring for an ethnically mixed child is problematic in terms of the binaristic black/ white division upon which social relations have historically insisted. As SuAndi's poem 'You'd Think That These Days You Couldn't Get Lost, But I am', points out, society's expectation of maternal – filial mirror imaging, or tracing 'the family face' is troubled, 'where no one looked like my mother/ and no one knew she looked like me' (p.74).

How does the child recognise herself in her mother? SuAndi, Kay and Onwurah demolish the toxic racialising residues of any skin-deep essentialism. The joy, reverence and attachment to the mother in their representations is profound where emotional identification and kinship are felt beyond the restrictions of social racialising processes. These are primary connections.

Space and Place
Until recently Britain's migratory narrative histories have tended to be overwhelmingly London-centric in commemoration, even though historically the ports in England, Scotland and Wales provided multiple points of disembarkation for people travelling to the British Isles (Southampton, Bristol, Cardiff, Glasgow, Liverpool, Gravesend, Dover). *The Story of M* is also contoured by migratory heritage and multiculturalism that is located in an urban setting that is not London. Specific streets in Liverpool and Manchester map M's family's locations. As Lynne Pearce notes, in her literary mapping of Manchester, "the street," "the district," and "the city" (2007:82) mark the contexts of habitation. In this respect the figure of M is a refreshing reminder of the regional yet cosmopolitan experiences lived beyond London in the post-war period, and she confirms her wholehearted affiliation with every district in which she lives, as her right of abode. Ash Amin explains that, 'the multicultural society characterized by everyday mixity', develops a civility born not of regard, but co-occupancy, and daily proximity – 'an unconscious cohabitation' – in a space, where 'there lingers another form of bodily judgment, equally unconscious, based on automatic coding … tapping into deep-rooted legacies of bodily judgment'. (2014: 102, 103) This is strikingly dramatised when M describes her brick fence, built to prevent the neighbour looking in on her, as retaliation to his racism – just as she resists the regulatory institutions of the State from the Church, to the Police to the NHS. As she fortifies her home against racism, she also fortifies her children with a pride in having inherited the ways, values, and means of her background.

There are further hidden heritages located in SuAndi's text that are also worth noting. M grows up primarily in the Catholic Church care home system– 'the only home I'd ever known,/ the orphanage.' (p.32)– after her father is lost at sea and her mother who, 'from the day he disappeared, she never/ got out of bed.' (p.33) In the 'care' of the nuns, women with babies were informed, 'your baby died / last night' but M realises eventually, 'All these babies – they weren't dying. / They were being given away for adoption.' (p.33) The latter-day revelations of the scandalous extent of the Catholic Church's callous mother-baby homes and forced adoptions system add further dimensions to what M has survived, and most importantly, what she does not replicate as she offers her own family love, security and indefatigable self-belief. However, the experience of being adopted or raised in care is not interchangeable with being of multi-ethnic heritage. Even though there is an over-representation of mixed children being left in the care system in contemporary Britain (Edwards, Ali, Caballero and Song 2012), the actual longstanding history of interracial families and their children in Britain should not be forgotten.[21]

Beyond the Text

While SuAndi's published drama evokes certain visual textual traditions pioneered by modernist and postmodernist writers and their experimentations with free verse and the 'look' of their poem or playtext on the page, it also contributes to a particular textual heritage that contemporary British writers of African origin have evolved. SuAndi's contemporaries Jackie Kay, Lemn Sissay, debbie tucker green, Patience Agbabi, Dorothea Smartt and Inua Ellams have developed uses of typographical, spatial and visual elements as intrinsic to the performativity of their monodramatic works' print layout. Further extending their poetic territories, SuAndi, Agbabi and Sissay also produce examples of what I have termed Landmark Poetics through inscribing and projecting poems on concrete material surfaces (pavements, sculptures, buildings, plaques, walkways, and clothing) rather than the pages of books.[22] Landmark Poetics combines artistic expression and social retrieval and represents the innovative ways in which black experience is restored to and momumentalised in British cultural heritage. (Osborne 2011) According to Maurice Merleau-Ponty, where language surpasses the limits of structure, (such as Landmark Poetics arguably does) it opens a 'new field of truths' and displays original thinking that breaks or rewrites the older contracts. ([1950] 1964:95) In *The Story of M* SuAndi achieves not only a 'new field of truths' in breaking down the relentlessly applied black-white binary but she also asserts a matrilineal *heritage* through the compelling theatricalised birthing of herself through her mother's legacy, as retold into the larger story of nation.

In rendering one woman's private history as a celebrated herstory, rescued from oblivion, *The Story of M* ensures that 'Audience members become the beneficiaries of this representation, occupying a key part in the retrieval/archival/revival process that creates artistic and cultural longevity.' (Osborne 2011: 235) It is a project of cultural reformation and renewal. As a text for the new EdExcel Examination Board's A-level in English Literature (from 2017), *The Story of M* will play a part in reworking the expectations of what gets taught in British secondary schools, just as the monodrama's content executes its own deconstruction of socially entrenched maternal and racial norms.

Obviously in publishing *The Story of M* as a book, a new method of engagement with it is engendered that is distinct from the sensory realm and semiotics created by its live production. The compilation of the book involves a process of organising the pictorial page space with the typographical layout of the spoken text (to be read), so that the accompanying multimedia performance materials are accommodated on the physical page in an act of (re)composition, as well as transcription from one dimension to another. This also brings into the same orbit, disciplinary differences for its critical reception and issues regarding longevity. The opportunities for conducting first hand performance analysis are limited. (Aston remains the work's premier source for performance studies scholarship.) SuAndi has been the drama's only performer to date.[23] Only one visual recording of it exists from 1995.[24] As dramatic literature in literary studies (where it has been the subject of PhD research and scholarly articles) the work has been primarily accessed as printed matter. In commemoratively bringing her mother to life through performing *The Story of M*, its future revivals will in all likelihood (paradoxically) rely upon reading about M from the page. Thus SuAndi retains her authorial control over her work's rationale to ensure a perpetual commemoration of her mother's life, as confirmed in the utterance, 'Hell, I wish you'd known my mother. / Oh, I forgot, you do now.' (p.55) Through effectively monumentalising the enduring power of Motherlove (in a world that continues to disenfranchise actual mothers socially, ideologically and economically), this Mothertext challenges the fixed typologies that continue to mark out certain citizens in oppressive ways, while also proclaiming 'the phoenix of the female spirit'. (p.60)

Endnotes

1. I employ the term monodrama to critically frame the distinctive solo performance writing authored by traditionally minoritised writers in contemporary British culture. As I have previously explored, monodrama performatively draws upon the legacy of the dramatic monologue as well as oral heritages of call and response, or the griot/te or confessional. (Osborne 2011, 2011a, 2013) It dramatizes a story not to be experienced in isolation, but against the backcloth of Britain's post-war social history with all the variegations of migratory, arriviste and indigene standpoints this elicits. Monodrama can activate different expectations for listener, reader, speaker and performer through the inter-compositional complementarity of poetry and drama. Contemporary examples include: Inua Ellams's *The 14th Tale* (2015) and *The Black T-Shirt Collection* (2012), Rahila Gupta's *Don't Wake Me: The Ballad of Nihal Armstrong* (2013), Cush Jumbo's *Josephine and I* (2013), Paterson Joseph's *Sancho: An Act of Remembrance* (2011), Mojisola Adebayo's *Moj of the Antarctic* (2008), debbie tucker green's *random* (2008), Lemn Sissay's *Something Dark* (2008), Valerie Mason-John's *Brown Girl in the Ring* (1999) and Sol B. Rivers's *To Rahtid* (1997).

2. In the selected further reading, readers can access an indicative range of women writers' literary creativities and the scholarship that has recognized and frequently retrieved it from obscurity.

3. The performative cannot divest itself of its historicity in culture or convention. As SuAndi has noted, 'I would say that 90% of my poetry isn't mine […] But because they're our stories, we can bring them out, dust them off, and do them again and again, or maybe rework them.' (Henry 2001:n.p.) In drawing upon Judith Butler's conceptual field, Sara Ahmed argues, 'If the performative opens up the future, it does so precisely in the process of repeating past conventions, as to repeat something is always to open up the (structured) possibility that one will repeat something with a difference.' (Ahmed 2014:93)

4. Examples of her poetry that render these groups of people can be found in: 'Darren', 'The Barmaid' and 'Just Slow' from *Nearly Forty*; '20-22 Hours From Blackburn', 'Passing', 'Sex, Love, Rape', her iconoclastic dramatic monologue, 'Playing for Life' in *Style in Performance*, 'Those Who Have Not Considered Living' in *There Will Be No Tears* and published in this volume, the affecting 'Aroma of Memory', an homage to 'ladies/of a certain age'. (pp.66-7)

5. Lauri Ramey observes, 'SuAndi is known for presenting an on-stage persona that is direct and sassy, wisecracking and poignant, political and opinionated, often controversial, and encompassing both history and topicality'. (2009: 292)

6. This note on terminology serves to anticipate any critical readers who require it. To counteract racism, and engender collective self-worth, the umbrella term 'Black' served as a unifying signifier throughout the 1970s and 80s for the multiple ethnicities racialised as 'coloured'. This collective identity politics enabled survival in a hostile surrounding society. Mixedness refers to multi-racial identity. It aims to undo the suggestion that there is a pure race as conveyed by the term mixed-race but of course is in itself imperfect as a descriptor. SuAndi eloquently positions herself in the maelstrom of terminology when she writes,

> As the daughter of a Liverpool Mother and Nigerian Father I meander between cultural tags including Mixed Raced, Black British, Nigerian and simply Black. It is the Black that I am most comfortable with which, well, seems ironic because my most successful writing has been based around my white mother and through her 'voice' the exploration of racism on family life.

'"Africa Lives on in We": Histories and Futures of Black Women Artists.' *Feminist Futures?: Theatre, Performance, Theory*. eds. Elaine Aston and Geraldine Harris. (New York: Palgrave Macmillan, 2006), 118–129, 123.

7. The range of critical material that explores the reach and complexity of black-centred post-war literary and theatre histories can be sampled in the work of: R. Victoria Arana, Colin Chambers, Kwame Dawes, Alison Donnell, Gabriele Griffin, Kadija George, Lynette Goddard, Corinne Fowler, C.L. Innes, Bruce King, John McLeod, Susheila Nasta, Birgit Neumann, D. Keith Peacock, James Procter, Mike Phillips, Lauri Ramey, Suzanne Scafe and Sara Upstone.

8. For further material indicative of the environment for black theatre at the end of the twentieth century see: Michael Billington *State of the Nation: British Theatre Since 1945* (London: Faber and Faber, 2007); Colin Chambers *Black and Asian Theatre in Britain: A History* (London and New York: Routledge, 2011); Clare Cochrane *Twentieth Century British Theatre: Industry, Art and Empire* (Cambridge: Cambridge University Press, 2011).

9. Sara Ahmed has theorised the relationship between emotions and speech acts in terms of labels that 'stick', see Chapter 4, *The Cultural Politics of Emotion* (2014).

10. The audience majority demographic in mainstream British theatre is invariably white, while for a black writer, the ideal audience could be imagined as a black majority. The anticipated audience (dependent upon venue and publicity) who turn up and the implied audience of the work's genesis can therefore lie somewhere between the real and the ideal of the writer's vision.

11. While women personae are her major focalisers, SuAndi's poetic-dramatic corpus is one that also recognises the involvement of fathers, brothers and sons in the lives of her women speakers. In this volume 'The Box' and 'Funny That' pay intimate tribute to the poetic persona's father as well.

12. In analysing the 2001 census, Charlie Owens reports, '661,034 people chose "Mixed", of which the "Mixed: White and Black Caribbean" category was the biggest mixed race group, followed by "Mixed: White and Asian", "Mixed: Other" and "Mixed: White and Black African"'. Moreover 'significant differences in age distribution are a clear indication that the mixed race group is a young phenomenon concerning children and young people' (Owens, 2008). A decade later, The Office for National Statistics identified a 7% increase in inter-ethnic couples in the 2011 census where, '1.2 million people (2% of the population) identified themselves with a mixed or multiple ethnicity, increasing from 660,000 (1%) in 2001. These Mixed/Multiple ethnic groups have the youngest age profile of all the ethnic groups' http://webarchive.nationalarchives.gov.uk/20160105160709/http://www.ons.gov.uk/ons/dcp171776_369571.pdf

13. The indispensible scholarship of Elaine Aston, Robert Crawshaw and Lauri Ramey approaches SuAndi's work from their respective disciplinary perspectives of feminist theatre studies, the sociology of literature and contemporary poetry and poetics.

14. To paraphrase Ifekwunigwe, the six areas are:

1. the formulation of a new lexicon to describe more appropriately, those people whose birth and 'blood' discomforts pre-existing sociological and anthropological groupings;

2. the creation of a non-hierarchical way of discussing difference to prevent colour-blind ideologies;

3. the addressing of 'psychosocial dynamics' between mothers deemed White and daughters deemed Black;

4. the use of the griot/te as a means of negotiating ethnographical tensions with orality and literacy;

5. the contesting of 'orphan consciousness' as delineating diasporic people's experiences;

6. to normalize the 'complex cultural realities' of mixed people in order to contest 'previous psychopathological and monolithic interpretations of experiences.' (Ifekwunigwe 1997: 128)

15. http://criticalpedagogies.com/2014/07/23/positioning-of-the-mixed-race-author-and-mixed-race-protagonist-in-british-childrens-literature/

16. Harpal Singh paraphrasing Gabriella Beckles-Raymond's paper, 'Mixed Race Masquerades: The Myth of Multiracial Harmony in Britain', in 'Conference Report, Critical Philosophy of Race: Here and Now', *Radical Philosophy*, 187 (2014): 64-66, 65.

17. These debates have been widely aired on social media, see http://www.mediadiversified.org for an important website of discussion concerning this topic.

18. Mother blame remains a toxic dynamic today by which women are socially and politically scapegoated, see Paula J. Caplan's *The New Don't Blame Mother: Mending the Mother-Daughter Relationship*, 2nd updated revised edition, (New York: Routledge, 2000). Arguably, *The Story of M* is a counter-discourse to Mother blame.

19. From a social sciences perspective Chamion Caballero continues the historicised foregrounding of positive, daily ordinariness in her research of the immediate post-war decades in 'From 'Draughtboard Alley' to 'Brown Britain': The 'Ordinariness' of Racial Mixing and Mixedness in British Society' (2012).

20. The film can be viewed on: http://player.bfi.org.uk/film/watch-body-beautiful-1990/ (accessed 29/12/16)

21. *The Story of M* is part of the literary corpus representing mixedness: novels: Caitlin Davis's *Family Likeness* (2013), Helen Oyeyemi's *The Icarus Girl* (2006), Diana Evans's *26a* (2005), Alex Wheatle's *The Seven Sisters* (2002), Joanna Traynor's *Sister Josephine* (1997), Bernardine Evaristo's *Lara* (1997), Laura Fish's *Flight of Black Swans* (1995); poetry: Jackie Kay's *The Adoption Papers* (1991); life writing: Jackie Kay's *Red Dust Road* (2010), Peter Frampton's *The Golly in the Cupboard* (2004), Michelle Scally-Clarke's *I Am* (2001) and Isha McKenzie-Mavinga's and Thelma Perkins's *In Search of Mr. McKenzie: Two Sisters' Quest for an Unknown Father* (1991); and plays: Nathaniel Martello-White's *Torn* (2016), Mojisola Adebayo's *Muhammad Ali and Me* (2011), *Moj of the Antarctic* (2008), Winsome Pinnock's *One Under* (2005) and Kwame Kwei Armah's *Fix Up* (2004).

22. SuAndi's Landmark Poetics include commissions for the poems inscribed in Manchester's first black public monument at Dulcie School (now demolished), 'Words on Discs' for Salford Wharf Centenary Walkway, Salford City Council, Salford Quays Project Office, at the Victorian Baths, Manchester www.victorianbaths.org. uk/documents/Women'sWalk (link no longer accessible) and for www.actsofachievement.org.uk/blackhistorytrail

23. SuAndi has designated Carla Henry who first played the Nurse as the only person appointed to 'play' M in the future when SuAndi no longer does.

24. Available from the Live Art Agency, *The Story of M* (1995) DVD, Ref. D2230. http://www.thisisliveart.co.uk/resources/catalogue/the-story-of-m1

SCENE ONE

Hospital room with a single bed with a screen to the side. A chair next to a small locker on which is placed a jug of water, tissues and a flower vase. 'M' is led onto the stage by a nurse; she is continuously coughing.

I've got cancer. I have.
Bloody cancer
And I know exactly when I got it –
eating a jam cream sponge cake
with my daughter's boyfriend.
I suppose you'll think I'm daft
Me calling him her boyfriend
what with him being gay!
But he is,
he's her boyfriend
and for me he's like a second son.
I was over at their place.
They live together.
Not together like,
But you know, together.
I was eating this jam cream sponge cake–
It was my first for months
I'd been dieting
Getting ready for her coming home.
I was born big – me.
Big!
Always was.
Take the time I tried to join the
Sally Army now you'll not believe this.
They wouldn't let me in
Because my legs were too big for the boots.
Christianity my big toe.
Hi get it?
Big toe, big foot, big leg,
Oh never mind

29

I'd lost two stone
thought it was a bloody miracle–
when suddenly
I get this massive pain
and wow cancer.
Think of all those cream cakes
I could have eaten.
Now I'm here, two parts dead.
Going over me life
like you do,
like you all will,
given the chance.

Not like poor Malcolm[1]–
No cancer for him–
Just a bloody racist
With a gun.
But for me–
it's a long drawn-out death.
And you'd be amazed
how those memories
come flooding back.

SCENE TWO

M sleeps (Nurse) picks up then drops a kidney tray.

Munitions?
All my friends worked in munitions[2],
but not me.
I've always been really sensitive to smells.
I was always passing out in church.
Used to drive the nuns crazy.

[1] Malcolm X also known as el-Hajj Malik el-Shabazz assassinated –
Feb 21, 1965

[2] Munitions: military weapons, ammunition, equipment, and stores

So I went into the laundries.
Loved it–
All that cleanliness,
Messing about with the suds.
Played bloody murder with your hands
And the heat could burn the end of your
nose off.
Anyways there I was this day
When the new chargehand goes past
And says, loud enough for me to hear like,
I bet this heat doesn't bother some people.
Them that belong in jungle!
Well bugger that. I was off.
The rest stayed, but not me.
I knew better.
There were folk from all over the world
Doing their bit for the war effort and here
was this fool talking about the bloody
jungle.
I bet he'd been no further than top of
the street.

Anyway –
I could wash at home
For my son and my husband.
Husband!
Bastard more like!
Don't get me wrong. I like men.
It took some time, I'll admit, what with me
being born a Catholic
And thinking any man, not wearing a
frock (a black frock naturally,) was
suspect.
I suppose that's why you never see
Jesus in trousers – because the Catholic
Church has spread so many stories
about the evil in them.

Well I found out the hard way.
I wasn't just naive,
I was thick.

First man that said he loved me, got me–
and not a wedding vow on his lips.
But being the Catholic that I was
I believed in the sanctity of marriage.
So I took him to court.
He was scared shitless!

The first day he stood in the dock
looking like the very criminal he was.
The next day he brought half the ship's
crew with him,
And they testified.
I'd been with them all.
A prostitute he called me.
Me! A Catholic girl, and the judge
believed him.
He looked at me as though I just stepped
off Lime Street.[3]
I cried;
I cried then. I really cried.
I had no one to turn to.
In the end I won the case,
But my son never took his name.
And I went back!
Back to the only home I'd ever known,
the orphanage.
Convent, more like!
I thought I'd had enough of nuns to last
me a lifetime, and then a bit more, and
here I was back with them.

They gave you another name,
A church name so to speak,
Like Sister Theresa or something.
Every morning, crack of dawn
They'd wake you

[3] The street is mentioned as the favourite haunt of prostitute "Maggie
May" in the Liverpool folk song of that name.

And tell you where you were working
that day.
And, they'd also pass out any special
announcements.
Like, Sister Theresa your baby died
last night.
Oh, and by the way, you're in the kitchen.
I'd pray every night that my son wouldn't die.
It took me ages to realise
All those babies – they weren't dying.
They were being given away for adoption.
And no one wanted a Black lad.
Well, Thank You Blessed Jesus.
But, I needed a husband,
A father for my son.

In those days my son
Was the only person I loved in the whole
wide world.
Loving a child is important–
I should know,
No one ever really loved me.

My mum had cancer and my elder sister.
For my mum they called it a broken heart.
You see, my father was lost at sea and
from the day he disappeared, she never
got out of bed.
I used to climb up to snuggle next to her.
Close – the way a cat does.
But if she realised it was me
She would shoo me away.
She didn't love me you see.
And I was the youngest.
I should have been loved the best.
They said, the day she died they found me
Lying right next to her cold dead body,
I must have been there for hours.
Neighbours took us in.

Neighbours!
An extended family, with no blood ties.
But they couldn't feed themselves
Never mind the three of us.
So, in time, the church took us.
Seems it was decided by some relatives
from across the water.
You can bet your life they didn't want us,
but they wanted to make sure we were
brought up as Catholics.
See what I mean. Christianity.
It's bloody stupid!

SCENE THREE

M is coughing really badly.

The priest's been round today with his
bloody rosary.
Telling me I should welcome death.
Welcome death!
I'd sooner welcome Margaret Thatcher[4].

My husband.
My ex-husband
Smokes 40 fags a day
And he's not got cancer.
He's an African.
A real African.
Not like me, a mix up of this, that, and a
bit of the other.
And the only good thing he ever did
for me

Was give me my daughter.
She's beautiful my daughter.
The day I got rid of him we had a party!
Bloody good riddance.

---

[4] Today this would be Trump that her mother wouldn't vote for

But he's a great father – always there
for her.
Buys her things; takes her out;
Loves her.
Maybe even more than I do
But as a husband,
well – he just another bastard man.
I met him on Berkley Street.

All the sailors lived on Berkley Street,
Sort of on top of each other.
Liverpool was great in them days.
It was like the world
You know,
People from all over the world
And we all lived happily
side-by-side.

I mean, I had names for the Chinese
That weren't,
Well you know,
Very nice.
I mean,
I didn't exactly
Call them Chinese.

But there again,
I don't suppose the names they called me
were very flattering either.
But we didn't beat each other up,
Shit, on each others' doorsteps.
Oh there were fights.
And name calling.
That made my mouth seem virginal,
And I'm sure there were many
Who would have liked to put us all
On our respective boats
and floated back home.
But in Liverpool 8,
You married anyone you wanted,

And no one gave a bugger;
So why the hell did I marry him?
I mean,
He didn't pretend to like my son.
He didn't even pretend to like me
But he still gave me my daughter.

Hulme
In the 50s
was just like Liverpool
On our street there was an Irish cobbler,
An African fish shop, and
Two funny French people
Who sold horsemeat to make stew out of.
No, not dog food, love, stew.
Where are you from OH!
Anyway, the grocers, the off licence,
And the people in the shop across the road,
They were English,
Or Scottish, or Welsh, or something.
Well, I mean, I can't tell,
can you?
We had Indians across the street
And Jamaicans round the corner.

But it was harder in Manchester;
You see, the war was over,
And the unity had gone out of our lives.
And I had become harder.
I don't mean, I was getting used to it
Just, that, well, I was getting used to it
And had to get harder.
Being spat on in the street!
Being turned away from rooms to let!
Not being able to get HP[5].
Hearing mothers tell their kids
Not to play with my kids.

[5] Hire Purchase: a system by which one pays for a thing in regular
instalments while having the use of it

Hearing their kids ask my kids
Why they were dirty.

I hit one kid once, outside church.
My daughter was like a flower,
All dressed up with long ringlets in her hair.
I made each of those ringlets, by hand,
every day.
I don't mean that weave on stuff like
they've got now,
It was her own hair.
And every morning I'd make her
stand there
As I tortured these ringlets into place.
Then out we'd go and some sod would
pat her head like she was an idiot
And they'd all fall out.

I was trying her out at a new
Sunday school,
As much as I hated the church,
And as much as the old fella should have!
We still wanted her to go.

Anyway, we were all stood outside,
Not together like.
The mothers and their kids over there,
And me and mine over here
When this spotty little four eyed creature
Comes up and says to my daughter,
If you have a wash next week
I'll be your friend and Jesus will love you.
Well, love that, I said,
As I slapped her across the mouth.
The police were called.
There was loads of trouble,
I had to go round and apologise.
I know I shouldn't have done it,
And if my daughter had been hit
I would have stabbed the lot of them.

But I was angry and hurting–
Hurting from the ignorance.
So when they decided to pull Hulme down,
I decided to move my kids
As far away from the likes of that as
possible.
So we moved to Ancoats[6],
A new council estate.

There were two blocks of maisonettes.
On the one side they were all dead smart.
Clean windows lace and ironed curtains.
On our side, there were a few curtains,
but mainly bits of cloth or nothing at all,
which didn't really matter
Because you couldn't see through the
windows for the muck.
Now, me,
I have always washed my windows.
And I change my curtains for Christmas,
Easter, Whitsun, Birthdays, and
sometimes
just when I feel like.
You see I'd reckoned that I couldn't
and didn't want to change black to white.
But people do judge books by their covers.
So I'd decided, long time back, that no
matter how badly off we might be.
Our home would be spotless and my kids
the same.

My daughter had all her clothes tailored.
Tailored.
And when I did buy I bought the best.
Her dresses came from this posh shop
on Stretford Road with a French name.

[6] Ancoats in Manchester has been called "the world's first industrial
suburb" its decline worsened following the 1960's slum clearance

Funny,
I can't remember the name now.
I was paying a fiver for her frocks,
Off-the-peg as they say
And it was only 1958.
Her shoes were leather,
her coats had fur trims in the winter,
And she always wore a hat and gloves.
What, me?
Me?
Well, I always wore a rain mac
And carried a plastic shopping bag.
But I was living for my daughter now.
When it came time for her to go to
Secondary School.
I hit a major problem.
The school uniform.
How in God's name
was I going to make sure
that everyone knew she was clean
each day?
Then one night I hit on this great idea.
I had the days of week,
You know, Monday, Tuesday
Wednesday, Thursday, Friday
Embroidered on the collar of her school
blouses, and every day she swapped a
cardigan for a jumper, you know.
You're laughing,
I'm laughing.
But it's not funny to be called dirty
and smelly.
So why are we laughing.

SCENE FOUR

The nurse has given M a bowl to vomit into – her weak state is becoming more and more apparent.

What was I talking about?
This chemotherapy is doing me head–
I told that nurse, I don't know about
getting rid of the cancer
Bloody hell
I'll tell you lot something,
Don't one of you take up hospital visiting
As a career –
For you're all bloody useless!
I was talking about the maisonette –
Good God, it's me that's dying, isn't it?

I'd been moving in, getting things ready
mostly during the early hours of the
morning.
I was working nights by then, in a canteen;
had been for a few years.

My son Malcolm,
well, he was away at Queens College
That's what we used to call prison–
I'd lost him to school expulsions,
Petty thieving, drugs, Nigger calling,
police beatings,
Do you think it was because of his colour?

I remember one time
I was working nights.
My daughter was about five or six
My son seventeen to eighteen,
He was supposed to look after her while
I worked.
I'd leave home at seven for a seven thirty
start and
get back around four in the morning.

This one day as soon as I turned into
our street
I knew something was wrong.
All the lights were on.
The house was ablaze like Christmas.
My heart started beating really loud
You know I could hear it.
When I got outside of the house
The front door was wide open.
I started to pray,
Pray for my daughter.
When I stepped inside the room –
It looked as though it had been raped!
My head was bursting,
All I could think about was her.
Was she safe
Was she safe?
I flew upstairs to her bedroom.
It was empty.
I must have started screaming.
I know I was making a noise but what
I was saying
I don't know.
I rushed out into the street
And the neighbour must have told me
The police had taken her.
So I ran.
I ran all the way from Hulme
To Moss Lane police station, and when I went inside
I saw her, sat on a bench
in her blue dressing gown and slippers with the red trim.
She had this look in her eyes.
I have never forgotten that look in her eyes.
It turned out they had been looking for my son.
Looking for something, found nothing.
So they took her instead.
"Home Alone", that's what they call it now, isn't it?
Oh, they hadn't tried to contact me.

Hadn't even contacted Social Services.
They just left her sat there, all night long.
She must have seen so much that night.
The thieves,
the drunks
the druggies
the prossies.
You see me,
I hate the police every last man of them.
And don't tell me they are here for my
protection.
I could tell you some stories about the
police,
About that caring arm across your shoulder,
then a hand slips down to your breast.
Or the reassuring pat on your knee that
travels up your thighs.
Yes, I could tell you stories,
But what's the point?
When my son was younger.
Not more than a toddler
I tried to do homework.

You know, work from home,
But I couldn't sew.
Couldn't do anything, really, but clean.
I couldn't cook either, much to the
annoyance of my husband.
So my homework was odd

There was this one time I made stuffed
straw dolls. The first day

These two huge bales of hay arrived,
And this bungle of rags
For the dolls' dresses.
I had to make fifty a day to get paid.
At the end of the first day there was
this thing.
It had half a head –

Drooping.
Two arms, no body, and one leg.
And its eyes popped off.
And the house looked like a romp in
a stable.
I had a right earful from the hubby for the mess.

Well, after that,
I cleaned other people's houses.
But they knew I needed the money,
So each day the lady of the house
Would increase the work.
First it was,
Could you rub this shirt through for my
husband?
Soon I was doing the whole family wash.
By hand!
For the same pay as I got for mopping
and dusting.
So the first chance I got to work in a
canteen
I took it.
And when the father left *(she waves)*
I washed those stacks of dishes with an
energy you wouldn't believe.

My daughter slept over with this West
Indian Family.
They were Jamaicans,
With three girls of their own,
So she was in good company.
Although I do wish they wouldn't tell
Those Tarzan stories about Africans,
She gets really upset.

Anyway, I was busy, as we were moving,
So every night after my shift
I'd get the all night bus from town and go
over to the maisonette to hang me
curtains or clean something.

The people living on the other side
Must have been really impressed
Thinking their own kind were moving in.
They must have been gob-smacked
to see us!
I heard one of them, you know the type,
Hair by mistake, make-up by necessity,
Asking my daughter when had she first
come to England.
Long before your lot, I yelled,
She slammed her balcony door
And we never spoke again.

Me and Anne West used to go shopping
together.
She lived next-door, Anne,
And didn't give a damn who you were or,
where you came from.
Her life had been too hard for snobbery,
And very soon it was going to get
murderously worse.
I don't know why I decided to move,
I'm sure some of it was instinct.
I had this fella by then,

He was Polish this fella and dead clever
with money.
His family had the lot; land, property, and
he was educated – that's how he got the
job as a wine waiter.
I don't mean he had studied wine
He bloody drank it,
You know, with his dinner.
He'd even got me sipping Drambuie.
Drambuie
It's dead posh that Drambuie.
Well, when the Communists took over
his country,

He came to England
And can you believe this
Just because he hadn't been educated
in Britain
They wouldn't let him work as a vet.
I told him
I wasn't surprised –
I'd seen it all before.
There are West Indians – university
qualified –
You know like teachers,
Driving bloody buses,
Believe me, I said,
As far as this country is concerned
If it's not bloody British it's shit.
Anyway it was him who convinced me to
buy somewhere.
I had no money, only me wages,
And no one was going to give me credit,
were they?
The only thing I could get on the tick
Was from the catalogue or Pauldens.
It's called Debenhams now.
In fact every thing we owned came from
Pauldens,
And one day my two complained so the
next Saturday I took them to town
To Lewis's.
We picked out this three-piece suite,
I didn't need it, like, but I had to make
them understand.
Then we went upstairs to the offices,
Filled the forms out and waited
For this snooty nosed bastard,
in his smelly suit, to tell me
That they didn't give credit to coloured
families,
And he was sure that I would understand.
Well, I didn't understand, but I did.

So George –
he was called George – did I tell you that?
He arranged everything
You know, like as though he was buying,
But my name went on the mortgage.
I'd pick the ones I liked from the pictures
And he'd go and look at them – and you
know, it was really strange,
But as soon as I got the one I wanted.
I wanted out of that maisonette.
I don't think we spent a year there.
And after all these years –
I still think about it.
Well, it could have been my daughter.

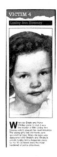

My little girl, but it wasn't, it was Lesley.
She was beautiful, Lesley.
Mum, can Lesley stay for tea?
Mum, I'm going to play with my friend
Lesley.
Lesley. Lesley.

10 second silent pause.

There were trees in Levenshulme
And at the back of our new house
a small garden
With a fence to one side
A wall on the other,
And one wall separating us from the garden
at the back.
Although we never went near the place,
Before signing the contracts,
They all knew we were coming.
Some of our stuff arrived on the back of a
lorry.
I kid you not, on the back of a lorry,
some in a mini van, a friend's car, a taxi,
and the rest by movers.

46

The old couple on the right
Never spoke one word to any of us
For the ten or more years we lived there.
The neighbours on the left weren't so bad,
Nosey like, but over the years–
we became sort of friends.
When we first moved in, my daughter
would leave the hall light on for me
coming home from work.
The grandmother remarked one day,
That maybe it was delight of having
electricity
That was making us so extravagant.
Silly cow.

But back to when we first moved.
On the first Monday.
The first Monday!
I done a bit of washing, curtains or
something.
I was hanging them out, as the house at
the back of us was having this tree
trimmed and heard them say to the bloke
doing the job
Don't cut the branches on that side,
I don't want those niggers
looking in on me.

By the end of the day
I had this f***ing big fence erected,
To stop that racist
Looking in on us.

So much happened in that house
As we laughed and argued
Through each day.
The world was changing too.
I remember when my nephew–
Have I told you about my family?

We're just like anybody
I mean, I'm not talking to that lot.
And wouldn't have them lot over
if you paid me!
But when my nephew was boxing[7]
at the Olympics games,
we watched every minute on the telly.
That's how we came to see it
Black Power against American racism.

My son Malcolm, had grown his hair,
he was reading the Solidad Brothers[8]
and quoting X.
We were always fighting, arguing.
Him screaming at me,
I've never cried so much in my life,
But I wanted him to grab a future,
to escape the life that was destroying him.
Sam Cooke[9] died and we played his music
late into the night. And I sang
won't somebody tell me what's wrong
with me–
why my life is so full of misery?
And I prayed that the woman found
with him wasn't white.
Much the same way as I tried to explain
to my daughter,
I prayed that the Yorkshire Ripper[10]
wouldn't be black.

[7] Alan Tottoh Welterweight 1944 – 2013

[8] Soledad Brother: The Prison Letters of George Jackson (1970). ISBN 1-55652-230-4

[9] Sam Cooke was an American singer, songwriter, and entrepreneur, January 22, 1931 – December 11, 1964

[10] English serial killer convicted of murdering thirteen women and attempting to murder seven others

A Black man and so many murders Would send people rioting
onto the streets, and many an innocent Black man
Would pay the price for one man's guilt. Oh, there's no
lynching in England
Here, they just beat you to death.

SCENE FIVE

*The nurse has removed M's dressing gown and slippers. She covers
M's head with a cap, ready for surgery.*

I'd do anything to be out of here,
out and about.
Not that I ever went anywhere.
When I first left the orphanage
I went into service, working for priests.
On the first night
I took a fancy to cold porridge.
So I nicked some. and propped myself up
in bed with a great bowlful.
The other maid just looked at me then
blew out the candle.
I didn't mind.
When we were kids
My sister worked in the kitchen cooking
for the nuns.
She used to sneak food in her
knickers and, along with our mate
Winnie, we'd eat it in the dark.
Anyway, the next night
I fancied porridge again.
So I nicked some more,
And the girl said,
Why are you eating that? she said
Why, because I fancied it. I said
Well don't, she said
Why not? I said,
Because the last girl that worked here, she said.

Ate porridge every night laced with arsenic
until she died.
I left the next morning.

We used to get one Saturday off per
month, in Service.
I used to meet my mates at Lime Street
to go to the matinees.
We would buy a great big bag of rotten
tomatoes
And go to see Arthur Askey[11].
Do you remember him?
I'm a buzzing, bloody buzzing,
busy bloody bee.
Well, buzz off, we'd say
And threw the buggers – then over the
road for Ken Dodd[12] with the other half.
Tight Ken we called him even then,
and we were right.
Mind you,
I wouldn't pay my taxes–
given half the chance.
That was it for me really.
As the years passed,
I'd spend my rare night off in front of the
telly, my feet up on a pouffe, eating a
cream cake.

I went on holidays.
I went to Paris once, –
in France!
It was marvellous.
Went to the Moulin Rouge
To see the Can-Can dancers.
And listen to this,

[11] English comedian and actor famous for *The Bee Song*

[12] English comedian, singer-songwriter and actor

when the girls kicked their legs up,
They had no knickers on!
Well, I started laughing
and when I laugh –
everyone knows about it.
I laughed so much they threw me out!

My daughter did the Can-Can once.
Over at the Lesser Free Trade Hall[13].
I sent her to dancing school
as soon as she could walk.
Well, I couldn't dance, so I just thought
that she wouldn't be able to either.
Well, what did I know about natural
rhythms, in any form,
If you get my meaning?
And she was a natural
She could do anything –
Tap,
Ballet,
Which amazed the teachers –
Well, African bottoms are not supposed
To be able to learn certain ballet techniques.
Bloody stupid if you ask me,
Well, you don't dance with your arse,
Do ya?

When she was thirteen
She auditioned and got a place
In the pantomime at the Palace Theatre[14].
When I went to collect her, after the first
rehearsal they told me, apologising,
Not to bring her back the next day.
They said she didn't blend in with the
rest of the kids.

[13] A Manchester public hall constructed in 1853–56

[14] Originally known as the Grand Old Lady of Oxford Street
Manchester, opened on 18 May 1891

Anyone try and tell me that now
I'd swing for them.
But that day–
I don't know.
I simply hugged her close.
and took her home.

I used to say to my daughter,
you're beautiful.
I don't mean on the outside
but on the inside.
And you have to remember that.
For so many people are going to try –
to prove different.
I'd tell her, wherever you go and you're
the only coloured person there.
I used to say coloured then.
Naturally I say black now.
Well, I'd tell her, you are representing
all black people,
so hold your head up high.

I'd say,
You see your father,
well, I can't stand the bastard.
But he's an African – that means you're
an African
never forget that.
I told my kids that I would always be
proud of them and hope that they would
never, you know, grow up and become
ashamed of me.
Kids!
Who'd have them?
Who'd be without them once they're here.

SCENE SIX

The stage slowly goes darker and darker.

Nurse, turn the light on.
I hate the dark.
Turn the light on.
She's useless that nurse. I've told her,
In the forties and fifties thousands of
qualified women
came over from the
West Indies to be nurses, and ended up
scrubbing hospital floors.
She'd be better off as a backing-singer.
Turn the bloody light on.
I'm scared of the dark.

SCENE SEVEN

BLACK OUT.

M rises and moves to the back of the room (stage) removing her gown and hat. As she does, she then turns to face her audience.

When my mother died, the world did not
stand still.
Nothing stopped, changed to note her
passing.
It was almost as though everything
moved at double speed.
She was there and suddenly, she was
this small container of ash,
And I could carry the whole of her
here in my hands.
When my mother died
No one felt the emptiness of life like I did.
Then, I don't know, weeks, months later
I woke up crying.
But in that moment
Between sleep and waking I began to laugh.

That dreadful laugh of my mum.
That laugh that said they won't keep us
down forever.
Then I began to remember her as she was
In private times,
Like how at the end of a day
she would come home
stand in front of the fire,
raise her skirt and pull off her corset,
scratching red welts into her skin.
I began to remember her stories,
tales of the convent.
Of her struggle to keep us proud of what
we were.
And wonder why she was always hopeful
that we would never be ashamed of her.
That day, I realised, that it's only the body
that dies.
But the spirit continues and you carry it
here, in this place of love.
And I laughed then at myself for
forgetting
that I carry the spirit of an ancestral
people,
Not only in the colour of my skin
But in my determination to see each day
through.
Better than yesterday.
And mixed in along with all those
Africans is this.
One special woman.

So, if any of you think that all mixed
raced people
Grow up confused, without identity,
Think again.

I work in schools,
And often, the cocky lad sat at the back

Asks me where I come from.
I answer, Manchester.
He'll say, Nope, where do you really
come from,
Manchester?
Why, where do you think I come from?
Somewhere hot and exotic he'll say
Well it's exotic in Manchester some days
well, I mean look at me.

Then there's the media,
desperate for a story,
Headlining,
The Mixed Heritage, confused shows.
They can F***
I know exactly who I am –
I am a Black woman
A mixed race woman.
I am proud to be a Nigerian daughter
whose father loved her.
He loved me so much,
And I am equally proud to be the daughter
of a Liverpool woman of Irish descent.

Confused? Get out of here.
If you're loved you are
Hell, I wish you'd known my mother.
Oh, I forgot, you do now.
For this was the story of M –
M for Margaret,
M for Mother,
And now M for Me.
And my name is SuAndi.

Catherine Ugwu and I commissioned SuAndi's *The Story Of M* in 1994 when we were running the Live Arts programme at the Institute of Contemporary Arts (ICA) in London.

When we took over the Live Arts programme in 1992 we approached it as not just a space to put on shows, but as a context to support the development of new and underrepresented artists, and to contribute to wider cultural discourses about the nature and role of contemporary art. We wanted to create programmes that responded to the practices and aspirations of black, queer, disabled, women and other culturally and socially marginalised artists, that were interesting and accessible to new and diverse audiences, and that provoked conversations. We were particularly concerned by the lack of contexts for, and awareness of, performance based work by black artists in the UK, and it was also important to us that we were not just programming existing work but were creating commissioning opportunities for artists to create new work. Key elements of the developments we put in place were two seasons devoted to a new wave of black artists from the UK and USA – *Respect* in 2003 and *More Respect* in 2004. *More Respect* was co-curated with Keith Khan and included work by Ronald Fraser-Munro, Chila Kumari Burman, Sarbjit Samra, Pamela Sneed and two new works commissioned especially for the season – Susan Lewis' *Ladies Falling* and SuAndi's *The Story of M*.

Since 1994 I have had the honour of commissioning many new works by many exceptional artists, but *The Story Of M* remains one of my proudest moments.

Lois Keidan, Live Art Development Agency, 2016

The Story of 'M' draws its energy and method from the oral traditions of Africa, Ireland and working-class communities across the UK. The printed text seems both a script *for* performance and a transcript *of* performance.

The presence of an audience is essential to the conversational method of the piece – its direct address uses satire, anecdote, humour, confrontation and unadorned human testimony to create an essential social, personal and cultural history. The piece involves that audience in a challenging and self-questioning dynamic. The result is a heightened dramatic tension that excoriates prejudice, celebrates resilience and repudiates self-pity and sentimentality.

The Story of 'M' enacts the experience of not one, but two characters, powerfully conjoined. By telling her mother's story and – simultaneously – her own, SuAndi subtly reflects the layers of experience that have accumulated around the complex cultural heritage of the UK and that entangle each successive generation.

It was this contribution to cultural life and understanding that earned SuAndi an honorary doctorate from Lancaster University in 2015. If ever there was a piece of theatre that embodies the dictum that we should learn from history rather than repeat it, then this is it.

Professor Graham Mort, December 2016

In addition to her work as a performance poet and with the National Black Arts Alliance, SuAndi has worked with a wide range of people, from university professors to convicted criminals, and from toddlers to senior citizens, from all racial and social backgrounds, using the arts as a vehicle for learning, understanding and experience across diverse communities. Her aims are to help heal wounds and eradicate misconceptions that can develop into blatant racism, and thereby empower individual self-worth. She has contributed to national and international forums and seminars in the arts, government, universities and the trade union movement; delivered workshops in galleries, youth clubs, primary and secondary schools, further education and in-service teacher education; developed performance scripts with prison inmates and expressive work with disenfranchised youth. As she says, 'I attempt to approach all my work not simply with a creative edge but also with a culturally innovative emphasis.' (SuAndi, private communication, 2016) Mick Wallis recalls a workshop SuAndi delivered to his students at Loughborough University in the 1990s:

> I was privileged to witness a skilled and utterly benign process of provocation. Through a fluid mix of questioning, attentive listening, and the occasional piece of poetry, SuAndi led the whole group into self-reflection, ethical judgement, and honest utterance. For many it was a precious moment of self-actualisation, inseparable from an understanding of difference and a watchful intolerance of prejudice.

**Mick Wallis, University of Leeds,
private communication, 2016**

SELECTED POEMS BY SuAndi

Women are indomitable people. This inner strength charges through the differences of race and culture. It doesn't matter whether or not we raise children, if we are single or living with a partner. What is remarkable is that it's the ordinary status of our lives that makes such huge and, in many cases, widespread and long lasting impact on the lives of others. Everyday someone will say I remember her, she...

Pankhurst, Gaskell, and Seacole – we know about them, there are volumes of print in their name. The women I honour and will continue to honour are the mothers, Sistahs and sisters, aunts, cousins and daughters who I pass each day. Countless numbers of them are strangers to me but I recognise in each and every one a determination. It is the phoenix of the female spirit that will always rise and like Sankofa[1] I will always remember to speak the names of other women gone to empower women of the future.

[1] *Sankofa* is a word in the Twi language of Ghana that translates as "Go back and get it"

WHAT DO MOTHERS WHISPER

What do mothers whisper?
as they coo
and cradle
inhale,
smell tiny fingers
stumpy toes
behind the ears, thighs
brushing their lips over eyelashes
of this small life
that she and he made out of love
lust
planned copulation
drunken thrust
all she ever wanted
never planned

But now in the silence
of her screams
pain forgotten
she says:

Do me one favour:
Don't die before me –
Survive!

HANDS

I have wrung my hands
soaked them in the dishwasher
cleansed them in the weekly wash
every Monday, Tuesday
a few extra things Thursday
just the sports kit Friday
and nothing for church, late on Saturday

I have sizzled them over frying pans
singed them with the Sunday roast
blistered their tenderness at almost every meal time

These hands have slapped out in the temper of concern
the sudden disappearance when my back turned

They have smoothed brows
and wiped away tears
over and over again

Late evening, they have tucked themselves under an armpit
or kept warm over the right – never my left – breast

They have sought out love
and been the security of simply crossing the road

Now I look at them
the nails are strong but plain
the palms still determined to be useful

So I wonder why
they move almost on their own
to hold my face and hide it as I cry.

NANDO'S[2]

I wonder where you are as we gossip:
the usual things – family, men!

Not one of you made a good choice:
Men are so stupid
a waste of space!

She will be different
But she pays the price

Dates are rare
so rare
I know each one:
no details
just the excitement of expectation

I wonder if you can feel jealousy?

She misses you just like me
more, of course

She looks so much like you
that every time she smiles
my heart cries

Then like you
she says something stupid:
Mum had such lesbian taste!

And I laugh so much I cry for real.

---

[2] *For Sophia Maxwell Yates in memory of her mum Yvonne Christian*

LADY MAKING

My mother bleached
kitchen tops
toilet bowls
curtain nets,
sheets that dazzled white
against the redness of her hands

Now I handle life in different shades –
the polished hue of manicured nails –
and thank my mother for all she did
to make a lady of her daughter.

THE TWIN

My mother had one
just the same

Not identical
naturally
thankfully

It wasn't that I hated it
but with the disdain of a teenager
I wanted it to be hidden
under wraps
constrained in public
whereas my mother favoured hers
with an affection of rubbing
and cooing in delight

Pampering Christmas-gifted talcum
the indulgence of cream cakes
and Bavarian slices
not to mention any-night fancied
Fridays fish and chip suppers

New Year barely passed before
Cadbury Cream Eggs supplanted
Duncan Walnut Whips

Click – click

Whereas I
her daughter
have endured, sacrificed
and denied
so many temptations

And in spite – yes! –
in spite of all my efforts
the bulge that rests arrogantly
beneath my breasts
is twinned in shape and form
to the stomach-bulge belly
of my mother's.

AROMA OF MEMORY

There are ladies
of a certain age
hair coiffured silver-grey to wig-black
or the corn-rolls of back-home childhood
that I hug

I smile, lean in
wrapping my arms across shoulders
once held straight
letting my hands travel
the spine of years

I breathe deeply the heavy perfume
of clean living
and a scent unnamed
that lingers in the smartness
of their clothes

In this moment
I am like a young buck
tempting this loveliness with
guile and flirtation
words that in their speaking
wash away the years
rekindling her bloom of youth

They giggle at my innuendo
a little naughty, never rude
for I am not church
no Miss-name falls from my lips

To me they are sweetness
'Sisters of Joy' to my vision

On a dull English morning
they are 'Praise to heaven'
for crossing my path
and the wickedness of accusation
that I have caught them slyly
heading to a discreet liaison

I tut-tut-tut my way through
this tête-a-tête
I have to avoid tasting them
my lips heavy with face powder
coconut lotion

I leave
waving away the greyness
of the day.

THE WIG

When the Chemo started –
courtesy of the National Health –
each woman was given a replacement
for her loss

My mother, Clairol-assisted by
'Nice 'n' Easy' over the years
weakened now by the ravages of radium
propped herself up and waited
and could not believe her ears when told –
lucky lady, still glossy and almost a full head –
that she wouldn't need hers

Bugger off! she said
finding a power we all thought had
dissipated through treatment

Did you think I've scrubbed floors
raised two kids
worked every hour God sends
laboured at overtime
and never once drawn Benefit
that I am going lie here
and be cheated out of what is by rights mine?

Then reached out to grab from the trolley
the closest one to hand, not caring one hoot
for its style, length or colour, shoving it almost
with the truculence of a child under her pillow
where I retrieved it and brought home
as testament to her life.

ALL YOUR FAMILY

I am your family

It wasn't the truth
or a lie, either

My father – her husband –
lived outside our days
by his own choosing
leaving mother and daughter
so different and similar

My mother fought for recognition
at parents' evenings
hospital appointments –
everywhere we went
together

I am your family
she told me
cursing the air she breathed
every time I risked my life
in the foolishness of late nights out
dangerous canoodling with boys too young
to make their own families

Saturday –
her one day of leisure –
I would watch and worry
that the swell of her breasts
and fullness of stomach
the pale alabaster of her skin
compared to the rich nutty brown of my own
might pass gene to gene to my slim form

I looked close and slightly disapproving

Now she is gone, left for ever
I find her in habits and rituals
I remember as hers
but now sit naturally as mine.

Alone I understand
I was loved totally by my mother
she was all my family.

EVERLASTING

I think of my mother when I'm
sleeping, talking, walking, thinking
eating, working, lazing doing nothing –
the same way you'll remember yours

Tears will dry
as the sorrow of these days moves
to memories of her laughter
and that tingle in your heart
is where she's planted her love

Everlasting.

THE BOX

I didn't keep it there:
in the beginning, I put it on a shelf

A lot of time passed
before I found the courage
to bring it home, then with no plans
I put it on the shelf, where it stayed
until an unexpected guest sent me scurrying
to freshen the spare room

How could I explain?
A heavy white cake-box?

I couldn't

I pushed it under the bed
to keep company with lost shoes
some single, without a partner
grey dust in blankets
without the energy to roll
warm, layered
a protection from the heaviest
of mattress rolls

I never took it out
never checked on its condition

But never forgot it was there.
moving from bed to bath
up and down the stairs

The white cake-box
haunted my thoughts
like a spirit on the landing

When Africa beckoned my return
going home
seemed close enough a home
to take it home

So down I went
my knees marked by the tufts of the carpet
my arms stretched far
until I pulled it close to me
stood, the cold box to my chest
my heart

Before I locked my luggage
I placed it carefully, secure under the zipper

In Ghana I walked a beach
of white sand damp with lapping blue
holding the box tight

As waves stroked my legs
I let the contents fall
and left my father in the sea
Floating home to Nigeria

FUNNY THAT

Old ladies tell me
I look like my mother
and I can see her perfectly –
love has etched her into my heart

When I think of who I resemble,
I see my father's hands
the fingers permanently bent
by concentration-camp cruelty
the skin shiny, taut like
deep brown leather

The hands move towards me
fingers trace the line of my eye
then a gentle descent down my cheek

He is looking for any sign that my stroke –
Bell's Palsy – is still obvious

At my mouth, he pulls tenderly
so my lips begin to open

My father leans forward and kisses my cheek
when he finds nothing, he smiles

I smile back
see my face reflected in perfect symmetry

Funny that
because old ladies tell me
I look like my mother.

YOU'D THINK THAT THESE DAYS
YOU COULDN'T GET LOST, BUT I AM[3]

You'd think that these days
you couldn't get lost

But I am

It's not just technology
maps are still useful
inked locations never fade
even when the lights go out
even in the dark there's a route
arriving somewhere
after you have left

When you left
I found myself
but when I looked about
I was lost

Being lost is like being suspended
in nothing
where everything has its own place
everybody has a place

Your place is empty

I can still hear my screams
five years old in the coat department
where no one looked like my mother
and no one knew she looked like me

Now my reflection is the only face I recognise
everyone else is different

Maybe I'm the alien –
a different species –
maybe this place is just one micro-second
behind where I should be

If I could meet myself coming back
I might arrive safely.

[3] Ekki múkk www.youtube.com/watch?v=2cAxLZpelmQ

SELECTED PUBLISHED WORK BY SuAndi

Poetry

- *4 for More.* (Manchester: artBlacklive, 2002).
- *I Love the Blackness of My People.* (Manchester: Pankhurst, 2003).
- *Kiss: Asian African Caribbean Chinese Love Poems.* (Manchester: Crocus, 1994).
- *Nearly 40.* (Manchester: Spike, 1992).
- *Style in Performance.* (Manchester: Pankhurst, 1991).
- *There Will Be No Tears: Selected Poems.* (Manchester: Pankhurst, 1996).
- 'Three Poems'. In *New Theatre in Francophone and Anglophone Africa.* ed. Anne Fuchs. (Amsterdam and Atlanta: Rodopi, 1999).

Libretto

'The Libretto of Mary Seacole'. In *Hidden Gems Vol II.* ed. Deirdre Osborne. (London: Oberon, 2012),

Selected Non-Fiction

Afro Solo UK: 39 Life Stories of African Life in Greater Manchester 1920–1960. Manchester: artBlacklive, (2014).
http://lascasbookshelf.tumblr.com/post/124500213237/free-book-afro-solo-uk-39-life-stories-of

In My Father's House (2007) http://www.blackartists.org.uk/wp-content/uploads/2009/05/imfhevaldocument.pdf

Book Articles and Online Talks

- *Acts of Achievement Colloquium* (out of print)
- *Unprecedented Times* for Black Theatre Network, USA NY/USA

- 'A message from SuAndi'. *Revealing Histories* http://revealinghistories.org.uk/who-resisted-and-campaigned-for-abolition/articles/a-message-from-suandi.html

- '"Africa Lives on in We": Histories and Futures of Black Women Artists.' *Feminist Futures?: Theatre, Performance, Theory.* ed. Elaine Aston and Geraldine Harris. (New York: Palgrave Macmillan, 2006), 118–129.

- SuAndi of National Black Arts Alliance on justice in arts funding'. Platform London, 28 Jan. (2015). http://platformlondon.org/2015/01/28/suandi-of-national-black-arts-alliance-on-justice-in-arts-funding/

- 'Cultural Memory and Today's Black British Poets and Live Artists', in *"Black" British Aesthetics Today* ed. R. Victoria Arana (Newcastle-upon-Tyne: Cambridge Scholars Press, 2007), 31-49.

- 'Eartha Kitt Once Told Me' in *Performing Poetry: Race, Place and Gender in Performance Poetry* ed. Arturo Cass and Cornelia Gräbner (Amsterdam and Atlanta: Rodopi, 2011), 219-28.

- With Michael McMillan 'Rebaptising the World in Our Own Terms: Black Theatre and Live Arts in Britain' in *Black Theatre: Ritual Performance in the African Diaspora.* ed. Paul Carter Harrison, Victor Leo Walker II and Gus Edwards. (Philadelphia:Temple University Press, 2002), 115-28.

- 'SuAndi'. The ASHA https://www.facebook.com/AshaCentre/

Selected Performed Work

The Calling. Libretto. BBC Philharmonic, London, 2005.

In My Father's House II Zion Arts Manchester 2004
In My Father's House. Contact Theatre, Manchester 2002.

Mary Seacole: The Opera.
Royal Opera House London Linbury Studio 3rd – 7th October 2000
Oct 9 at 20:00, Oct 11 at 14:00 and 20:00
Bridgewater Hall, Manchester, 2003.
Bernie Grant Arts Centre London 4th – 5th October 2007
Sugar & Spice Festival, Gateshead, U.K.
Seacole Extract Productions:
Jamaican Embassy
Battersea Arts Centre

Revelations of Black. Royal Exchange Theatre, Manchester Festival, 1985.

The Story of M. Premiere performance Institute of Contemporary Arts, London, 1995.
Directing advice original production Bush Hartsorn
Technical advice Steve Bryan

Television
Revelations Are Black. Channel 4, (1997).
http://www.camoci.co.uk/video/suandi/revelations%20suandi.mpg

WORKS CITED and INDICATIVE FURTHER READING

Adorno, Theodor. *Aesthetic Theory* trans. and intro. Robert Hullot-Kentor (London: Athlone Press Ltd, 1997).

Ahmed, Sara. *The Cultural Politics of Emotion* [2004] 2nd edition, (Edinburgh: University of Edinburgh Press, 2014).

Amin, Ash. 'Ch.6', *Conversations in Postcolonial Thought* ed. Katy P. Sian (New York: Palgrave Macmillan, 2014), 95-104.

Arana, R. Victoria. ed. *"Black" British Aesthetics Today* Newcastle-upon-Tyne: Cambridge Scholars Press, 2007.

-----. and Ramey, Lauri. eds. *Black British Writing* (New York and Houndsmill, Basingstoke, Hampshire, England: Palgrave Macmillan, 2004).

Aston, Elaine. 'A Critical Step to the Side: Performing the Loss of the Mother.' *Theatre Research International,* 32:2, (2007): 130-42.

-----. *Feminist Views on the English Stage: Women Playwrights, 1990–2000* (Cambridge: Cambridge University Press, 2003).

Bakhtin, M. M. 'Discourse in the Novel', in Holquist, M. (ed.), C. Emerson and M. Holquist (trans.) *The Dialogic Imagination: Four Essays.* (Austin: University of Texas Press, 1981).

Barker, Howard. *Arguments for a Theatre* (Manchester: Manchester University Press, 2nd ed., 1993).

Barn, Ravinder. and Harman, Vicki. eds. 'Mothering Across Racialised Boundaries', Special Issue, *Ethnic and Racial Studies,* 36:8, (2013).

Bland, Lucy. 'White Women and Men of Colour: Miscegenation Fears in Britain after the Great War.' *Gender and History,* 17:1, (2005): 29–61.

Byron, Glennis. *Dramatic Monologue.* (London: Routledge, 2003).

Caballero, Chamion. 'From "Draughtboard Alley" to "Brown Britain": The "Ordinariness" of Racial Mixing and Mixedness in British Society', in *International Perspectives on Racial and Ethnic Mixedness and Mixing* ed. Rosalind Edwards, Suli Ali, Chamion Caballero and Miri Song (New York and London: Routledge, 2012), 36-56.

-----. and Edwards, Rosalind. *Lone Mothers of Mixed Racial and Ethnic Children: Then and Now* (London: Runnymede Trust, 2010). Can be downloaded at http://www.runnymedetrust.org/uploads/publications/pdfs/LoneMothers-2010.pdf

Carleton, Frances Bridges. *The Dramatic Monologue: Vox Humana.* (Salzburg: Institut für Englische Sprache und Literatur, 1977).

Crawshaw, Robert. 'Translating the In-Between: Performance Poetry and the Relationship Between Language, Literature and Society' in *From Literature to Cultural Literacy* ed. Naomi Segal and Daniela Koleva. (Houndsmill, Hampshire and New York: Palgrave Macmillan, 2014), 106-121.

-----. http://www.bbawriting.com/suandi/

-----. 'Translating the In-Between: SuAndi's *The Story of M* or Reflections on Sociological Approaches to Literary Analysis' Unpublished paper, Gesellschaft übersetzen conference, University of Konstanz, 29-31 October, 2009.

Culler, A. Dwight. 'Monodrama and the Dramatic Monologue.' *Publications of the Modern Language Association,* 90:1 (1975): 366–385.

Curb, Rosemary K. 'Re/cognition, Re/presentation, Re/creation in Woman-Conscious Drama: The Seer, The Seen, The Scene, The Obscene.' *Theater Journal,* 37:3 (1985):302-316.

Evaristo, Bernardine. 'Going it...alone: solo performers – the art and the ache'. *Artrage* (November 1994): 14-15.

Fowler, Corinne and Pearce, Lynne. ed. *Postcolonial Manchester: Devolved Literary Cultures* (Manchester University Press, 2013).

Fuchs, Anne. '"I'm a Very Northern, Mixed-Race Woman": An Interview with SuAndi' in *Staging New Britain: Aspects of Black and South Asian British Theatre Practice* ed. Geoffrey V. Davis and Anna Fuchs (Brussels: Peter Lang, 2006), 205–217.

Goddard, Lynette. *Staging Black Feminisms: Identity, Politics, Performance* (London: Palgrave Macmillan, 2007).

Goodman, Lisbeth. *Feminist Theatres: To Each Her Own* (London and New York: Routledge, 2003).

Harris, Angela P. 'From Color Line to Color Chart: Racism and Colorism in the New Century', *Berkeley Journal of African-American Law and Policy,* 10:1 (2008): 52-69.

Henry, Carla. 'Transcription 2001', in *4 For More* ed. SuAndi (Manchester: Black Arts Alliance, 2002), n.p. Hinton, Laura, and Hogue, Cynthia, eds. *We Who Love To Be Astonished:*

Experimental Women's Writing and Performance Poetics. (Tuscaloosa and London: The University of Alabama Press, 2002).

Ifekwunigwe, Jayne O. 'Diaspora's Daughters, Africa's Orphans?: On Lineage, Authenticity and "Mixed Race" Identity' in *Black British Feminism* ed. Heidi Safia Mirza (London and New York: Routledge, 1997), 127-152.

Karavanta, Mina. 'SuAndi's *Mary Seacole*: A Hybrid Cartography in Libretto' in *Hidden Gems Vol. II* ed. Deirdre Osborne (London: Oberon Books, 2012), 323-29.

Kaynor, Gad. 'The Actor as Performer of the Implied Spectator's Role.' *Theatre Research International*, 22:1 (1997): 50-63.

Kumamoto, Chikako D. 'Bakhtin's Others and Writing as Bearing Witness to the Eloquent "I."' *College Composition and Communication*, 54:1 (2002): 66–87.

Langellier, Kristin M. 'Personal narrative, performance, performativity: Two or three things I know for sure.' *Text and Performance Quarterly*, 19:2 (1999):125-144.

Lejeune, Philippe. *On Autobiography.* ed. Paul John Eakin. Trans. Katherine Leary. (Minneapolis: University of Minnesota Press, 1989).

Merleau-Ponty, Maurice. *Signs* (1950), translated by Richard C. McCleary (Chicago: Northwestern University Press, 1964).

Mix-d Museum http://www.mix-d.org/museum/

Munden, Paul. and Wade, Stephen. eds. *Reading the Applause: Reflections on Performance Poetry by Various Artists* (New York: Talking Shop, 1999).

Okojie, Irenosen. 'British black writers: we're more than just Zadie Smith and Monica Ali' http://www.theguardian.com/commentisfree/2014/mar/23/black-british-writers-more-than-zadie-smithmonica-ali

Olumide, Jill. *Raiding the Gene Pool: the Social Construction of Mixed Race.* (London, Sterling Virginia: Pluto Press, 2002).

Osborne, Deirdre. ed. *The Cambridge Companion to British Black and Asian Literature (1945-2010)* (Cambridge: Cambridge University Press, 2016).

----. 'Skin Deep, a Self-Revealing Act: Monologue, Monodrama, and Mixedness in the Work of SuAndi and Mojisola Adebayo.' *Journal of Contemporary Drama in English* 1.1 (2013): 54-69.

-----.'The Body of Text Meets the Body as Text: Staging (I)dentity in the Work of SuAndi and Lemn Sissay.' *Crisis and Contemporary Poetry.* ed. Anne Karhio, Seán Crosson and Charles I Armstrong. (London: Palgrave Macmillan, 2011a), 230-47.

-----. '"Set in Stone": SuAndi and Lemn Sissay's Landmark Poetics' in *Performing Poetry: Race, Place and Gender in Performance Poetry* ed. Arturo Cass and Cornelia Gräbner (Amsterdam and Atlanta: Rodopi, 2011), 197-217.

Owens, Charlie. in Lise, Marcia. (rapporteur) ESRC Series, Seminar 1:*Spaces and Places* 12 December 2008, London South Bank University.

Palko, Abigail L. *Imagining Motherhood in Contemporary Irish and Caribbean Literature* (NewYork: Palgrave Macmillan, 2016).

Pearce, Lynne. 'Women Writers and the Elusive Sublime: the View from "Manchester, England".' *Contemporary Women's Writing,* 1:1/2, (2007): 80-97.

Preston, Carrie J. *Modernism's Mythic Prose: Gender, Genre, Solo Performance.* (Oxford: Oxford University Press, 2011).

Ramey, Lauri. 'Contemporary Black British Poetry as a Diasporic Avant-Garde.' in *Diasporic Avant-Gardes: Experimental Poetics and Cultural Displacement,* ed. Carrie Noland and Barrett Watten. (New York: Palgrave Macmillan, 2011), 189-206.

-----. 'SuAndi' in *Dictionary of Literary Biography: Twenty-First-Century "Black" British Writers* ed. R. Victoria Arana (Sumter, South Carolina: Bruccoli, Clark, and Layman; & Detroit, Michigan: Gale Research Company, 2009), 291-8.

-----. 'Performing Contemporary Poetics: The Art of SuAndi and Patience Agbabi' in *Contemporary Black British Women's Writing,* Special Issue of *Women: A Cultural Review* ed. Deirdre Osborne, 20:3, (2009a): 312-22.

Rich, Adrienne. *Of Woman Born: Motherhood As Experience and Institution* (London: W.W. Norton and Company Ltd., 1977)

Ricoeur, Paul. *Oneself as Another*. Trans. Kathleen Blamey. (Chicago: University of Chicago Press, 1992).

Severin, Laura. *Poetry off the Page: Twentieth-Century British Women Poets in Performance*. (Aldershot: Ashgate, 2004).

shange, ntozake. *For colored girls who have considered suicide when the rainbow is enuf.* (New York: Macmillan, 1977).

Sinfield, Alan. *Dramatic Monologues*. (London: Methuen, 1977).

Sleeman, Elizabeth. ed. 'SuAndi' in *International Who's Who in Poetry* (London: Europa Publications Ltd, 2003), 315.

Smith, Sidonie. 'Identity's Body.' *Autobiography and Postmodernism*. ed. Kathleen M. Ashley, Leigh Gilmore, and Gerald P. Peters. (Amherst: University of Massachusetts Press, 1994), 266–292.

Tabili, Laura. 'Women "of a Very Low Type": Crossing Racial Boundaries in Imperial Britain.' *Gender and Class in Modern Europe*. ed. Laura L. Frader and Sonya O. Rose. (Ithaca: Cornell University Press, 1996), 165–190.

Tizard, Barbara. and Phoenix, Ann. *Black, White or Mixed Race: Race and Racism in the Lives of Young People of Mixed Parentage* (London and New York: Routledge, 1993).

Twine, Frances. W. *A White Side of Black Britain: Interracial Intimacy and Racial Literacy* (Durham: Duke University Press, 2011).

Ugwu, Catherine. 'Keep On Running: The Politics of Black British Performance.' *Let's Get It On: The Politics of Black Performance*. ed. Catherine Ugwu. (London: Institute of Contemporary Arts, 1996), 54–68.

Wallace, Clare, ed. *Monologues: Theatre, Performance, Subjectivity.* (Prague: Litteraria Pragensia, 2006).

Wilson, Anne. *Mixed Race Children: A Study of Identity.* (London: Allen and Unwin, 1987).

Worthen, W.B. *Drama: Between Poetry and Performance* (Chichester, West Sussex: Wiley-Blackwell, 2010.

SuAndi has always combined her life as a writer with her freelance role as Cultural Director of NBAA National Black Arts Alliance the UK's largest network of Black artists. Since 1985 she has organized exhibitions, performances, seminars, colloquiums and workshops in schools and prisons. She is a sought-after speaker for conferences in the UK and internationally.